PAT SPRINGLE

UNTANGLING RELATIONSHIPS

LEADER'S GUIDE

A Christian Perspective on Codependency

Susan A. Lanford

Introduction

Leading an *Untangling Relationships* Group

This course is not a typical Bible study in which the lecture method is the primary teaching tool. In fact, some of your church's best Bible teachers may not be qualified to lead a discovery group because they might not possess some of the very important skills listed below. The discovery group leader guides the group process, allows group members to share information and insights, and assists members ready to identify and explore their own feelings about certain issues that the discussions prompt.

Important spiritual qualifications for a discovery-group leader are to—

be a growing Christian with a personal relationship with Jesus Christ;
be a person of prayer and daily Bible study;
be an active member of a local church;
have a sense of God's call to the ministry of support groups;
be spiritually gifted for the work;
have a commitment to confidentiality within the cup;
be willing to give time and energy to help group members;
have a teachable spirit;
be sensitive to the daily leadership of the Holy Spirit;
love the Lord and love people.

Persons who have led groups through *MasterLife Disciple's Prayer Life* or *Experiencing God* have a strong spiritual foundation for leading discovery groups. *LIFE Support Leader's Handbook* (The Handbook can be downloaded at no charge from http://www.lifeway.com/download.asp.) and *WiseCounsel: Skills for Lay Counseling* (0767326156) are strongly recommended as resources for potential discovery-group leaders. These two resources address every issue you will need for conducting this study.

Steps for Starting an *Untangling Relationships* Group

The following steps can help you prepare to minister effectively through this discovery group.

Check each of the following steps as you complete them:

❑ Prayer
❑ Selecting the group's leader
❑ Enlisting an apprentice
❑ Understanding foundational concepts of discovery groups
❑ Determining the logistics
❑ Ordering materials
❑ Setting fees
❑ Determining child-care arrangements
❑ Promotional efforts
❑ Getting started
❑ Requesting Church Study Course credit

Group Session 1

Understanding Codependency

Session Goals

This session is designed to help members—
define codependency and describe the effects of codependency in a person's life;
review God's plan for family life;
affirm for each person the importance of feeling loved and valued;
begin the process of knowing other group members and learning to trust them.

Before the Session

❏ Read and complete the learning activities for unit 1 in Untangling Relationships member's book.
❏ Find a quiet time and place to pray for group members by name. Ask the Lord to give you the wisdom you need to prepare for and lead the group session.
❏ Read the "During the Session" section which follows. This section suggests more activities than you likely can cover during the time allotted. Select the activities that best suit your group members' learning needs. Feel free to adapt or develop other activities you believe will best help your group members benefit from their study of unit 1.
❏ Decide on the amount of time you want to allow for each activity. Activities are set up here for a one-and-a-half-hour format. Adjust time frames as necessary to accommodate the time you have allotted for a session. As a reminder during the group time write in the margin of this guide the adjusted times. Always be prepared to change your plans as the Holy Spirit leads you and as the needs of the group or an individual dictate.
❏ Arrange in a circle only enough chairs for each member and for yourself.
❏ Display on a poster or chalkboard the unit memory passage:
The LORD sustains all who fall, And raises up all who are bowed down. The LORD is near to all who call upon Him, To all who call upon Him in truth.
—Psalm 145:14,18
❏ For the introductory activity gather a variety of game pieces from different board games. On two tables in the room set a playing board with unrelated cards and game pieces. Around each table place four chairs.
❏ Place markers and name tags near the door.
❏ Make two sentence strips which say: "Why am I here?" and "What personal goal can I accomplish by being here?"
❏ From brightly colored paper cut out the numbers 1, 2, and 3. Make these numbers large enough in height and width so you later in the session can write on them several words.
❏ Duplicate Worksheet I for use in the small-group sharing time.

Allowing members to share freely during group sessions is far more important than is sticking legalistically to a plan for the group session you develop before the session begins. Group members sometimes come to the sessions absolutely bursting at the seams to share something that happened in their lives during the previous week that relates to the week's content. Be sensitive to this need, and be flexible.

During the Session

Introductory Activity (15 minutes)

1. Greet your newly enrolled group members as they arrive. Invite each one to make a name tag. As members arrive, introduce each one to the others in the room.

2. As the first two members arrive, invite them to sit at one game table. Give them these simple instructions: "We have a few minutes before we start; please enjoy playing this game. It takes only one minute to complete one game." As the two members begin to study the game board and begin to realize that its pieces clearly are unrelated to each other, they obviously will be confused. They may begin to make remarks like, "Wait a minute. These are pieces to a Clue game on a Monopoly board. We can't play this." Even though you are aware that what they are saying is true, merely smile and encourage them to enjoy the game.

As the next two group members arrive, ask them to sit at the second game table. Give them the same instructions as you gave the first two members. After one minute passes, send to each table two additional players who have arrived.

You may have more members of your group than you have chairs around the tables to seat them. If so ask those who are not seated to observe the game players for a few minutes until the session starts.

3. When your starting time for the session arrives, call everyone to the circle of chairs. Be sure all group members have met one another.

Ask group members to describe their dilemmas as they played the introductory games. Affirm each answer.

Then say: "You face another dilemma tonight. Trying to play games without rules and without order may be symbolic of some questions you have tonight. You may be trying to answer the questions: 'Why am I here?' and 'What personal goal can I accomplish by being here?' (Display the sentence strips with these questions.) Begin now thinking about those questions; we'll discuss them in a few moments."

Finally, as a way to introduce the content of the session, remark that codependents face a major dilemma, too. Ask group members to turn to the last comment in the left margin on page 10 of *Untangling Relationships: A Christian Perspective on Codependency* and underline it.

Tell the group members: "The dilemma for codependents is that they feel trapped and hopeless. We are in this group to understand better this dilemma and eventually to learn the differences between surface solutions and lasting solutions to the problem of codependency."

Stress that understanding this matter will take time. Emphasize that group members will make a journey together to obtain this type of understanding. Share with group members the reasons why you believe that people will benefit from journeying in the company of other dedicated discoverers.

4. Lead the group in prayer. In your prayer acknowledge the dilemmas group members faced tonight—both literally and symbolically—and will face throughout the course. Thank God for bringing the group members together and for giving them a task. Praise Him for His presence, and invite the Holy Spirit to be the Teacher for every session.

Group Sharing Time (35 minutes)

1. Ask members to turn to page 27 of *Untangling Relationships*. Tell them they can use answers they recorded on page 27 to help answer the two questions, "Why am I here?" and "What personal goal can I accomplish by being here?" posed earlier. To answer the question: "Why am I here?" invite members to share which boxes they checked in the activity the middle of page 27. Then, to answer the goal-related question, invite members to pull out the separate piece of paper they used during the study to record a goal. Let those who are willing state their goal aloud, and then collect the pieces of paper on which they recorded this information earlier. Thank group members for the information, and assure them that by having this information you can pray for them better during the next few weeks.

2. Ask members to pull out the group covenant they discussed at the introductory meeting and reread it in light of the goal they just recorded. Invite any additional discussion of the covenant which will assist group members to meet their goals and will help them to participate fully in the group experience.

3. Identify another dilemma facing group members in this first session. This dilemma involves the fact that members have feelings ranging from curiosity all the way to fear about other members in the group and what compelled these others to join. Explain the distinct types of persons who join this type of discovery group:

    1) Some want to learn more about codependency in general. They may understand that codependency is a condition that affects many individuals in the world today and may feel that they could benefit from some objective knowledge about it.
    2) Some do not know the word codependency but identify closely and personally with the title of the materials, *Untangling Relationships*. They may think they would like to improve relationships in which they are involved, and they think this course might help.
    3) Some know they have or are struggling with codependency issues and want to work on those issues.
    4) Some suspect they know friends, family members, or even fellow church members who they believe are codependent. These group members want to learn how to relate better to codependent individuals.

Say: "Tonight you may feel that you represent one of these four types, but several weeks into the course your assessment of which of these four types you are may change. Deciding which type of person you are is not as important as is keeping your mind and heart open to the content present in each unit and to each other in each group session. Because some of the key issues of codependency—control, guilt, and loneliness—are basic human issues, each person will find a point of personal identification with codependency, even if you conclude you are not actually a codependent."

4. Mention how appropriate you feel this unit's memory passage is to anyone who has faced difficulty in life. Ask anyone willing to recite this passage from memory to do so. Call group members' attention to the poster showing the memory passage; ask group members to identify one word in the passage which is most meaningful to them.

5. Spend time exploring the roots of codependency in dysfunctional families. Ask members to turn to page 12 of their member's book and circle or highlight the boxed definition. Then, refer to the boxed exercise on page 15 to summarize God's intention for family relationships. Invite members to share examples of healthy traits they recorded in the right column of the box.

Refer to the "Signs of Functional Families" on page 16, and ask for three volunteers. Distribute to each volunteer the cut-out numbers you prepared in advance along with a pen or pencil.

Start volunteers at different points in the circle, and ask them to write down the various responses of the group members. The volunteer holding the number 1 will ask each group member to tell which quality on page 16 he or she ranked #1; the volunteer will record each answer on the cut-out number 1. The volunteers holding the number 2 and the number 3 will do the same with the group members' second and third choices.

When each volunteer finishes polling the group, display the numbers and discuss the answers. Be sure group members circle or highlight the last paragraph in this section to understand better the roots of codependency.

6. Turn to the examples of dysfunction listed on page 18 of the member's book. Ask group members to tell, without sharing names, how many of the stories listed there they associated with people they know.

Discuss thoroughly the material and exercises related to Deuteronomy 5:9-10 which follow on pages 18-19 and which occur in the middle of page 21.

Conclude this discussion by reminding group members about the hope each family has through Christ to interrupt the patterns of dysfunction in its past and present.

Small-Group Sharing Time (25 minutes)

1. Inform group members that each group session will include a time of small-group sharing. Tell them you will not be a part of a small group but will be available to any small group that needs a moment of help or input from you. Ask the group members to divide into groups of two or three and to pull their chairs together.

2. Distribute Worksheet 1 which lists small-group steps. Talk through the instructions, clarify any point that is unclear, and invite small-group members to begin talking. Ask the person in each group who is sitting closest to you to begin.

3. After 10 minutes, call time, and ask group members to move their chairs to form one large circle again.

Closure (15 minutes)

1. Hear from each group reports on steps two and three.

2. Invite a member to share the unit's key statement he recorded at the bottom of page 27. Thank group members for their preparation through study and their participation during the group session.

3. Preview unit 2 briefly. Point out an extra writing assignment on page 51 in which members are asked to describe how their relationships with their fathers and mothers have shaped their perceptions of God. Tell members that this writing assignment will be important as they prepare for the next group session.

4. Stand and join hands in a prayer of dismissal. Ask members who choose to do so to voice a one-sentence prayer committing themselves to God's purpose for the duration of the group.

After the Session

❏ Write down each group member's name. Before the next group session pray for each member specifically. Pray especially for group member with special needs.
❏ Call each group member; encourage him or her in the study of unit 2. Thank each group member for his or her commitment to the group.
❏ Make a copy of the leader worksheet, "Evaluating Each Session." Use this to assess the first session. If you have an apprentice, fill in and discuss this worksheet with him or her.
❏ Read "Before the Session" for Group Session 2 (on the following page) to evaluate the amount of preparation you will need for your next group session. At the top of the Group Session 2 material record when you will do your preparation.
❏ Carefully study unit 2 and do all the exercises in the member's book.

Group Session 2

Lack of Objectivity

Session Goals

This session is designed to help members—
understand better the source of a codependent's lack of objectivity;
explain five defense tactics which codependents use to avoid painful reality;
discuss examples of "blinders" codependents use to keep from facing reality;
reflect on this unit's exercises that called for objectivity.

Before the Session

❑ Read and complete the learning activities for unit 2 in the *Untangling Relationships* member's book.
❑ Find a quiet time and place to pray for group members by name. Ask the Lord to give you the wisdom you need to prepare for and lead the group session.
❑ Read the "During the Session" section which follows. Select the activities that best suit your group's learning needs. Feel free to adapt or develop other activities you believe will best help your group members benefit from their study of unit 2.
❑ Decide on the amount of time you want to allow for each activity. Activities are set up here for a one-and-a-half hour format. Adjust time frames as necessary to accommodate the time you have allotted for a session. As a reminder during the group time write in the margin of this guide the adjusted times. Always be prepared to change your plans as the Holy Spirit leads you and as the needs of the group or an individual dictate.
❑ Arrange in a circle only enough chairs for each member and for yourself.
❑ Arrange a poster board or bulletin board near the entrance to your room.
❑ On a chalkboard, write the following instructions for the introductory activity:
   Welcome back
   • Recall a time when you were physically, temporarily blinded (such as a power outage, a snowstorm, in a subterranean cave, etc.). Find one other group member and describe your experience to this person. Then, tell this person what being blinded felt like and what regaining your sight felt like.
   Continue to swap stories until starting time.
   Enjoy!

Remember that these activities are to assist you as you lead the group. Your group may desire and need to use a more simple format in which group members simply share how the study is impacting their lives. Your prayer and preparation will free you to assist the group process with learning activities as needed.

During the Session

Introductory Activity (20 minutes)

1. Greet all members by name as they arrive. Help them find their name tags from last week, or make new ones.

2. Ask members to pin or tape to the poster board or bulletin board the articles they clipped for the exercise on page 40 of the member's book.

3. Point out the directions written on the chalkboard about times group members were blinded. Encourage group members to share these experiences with each other until time to begin.

4. Ask everyone to return to the circle of chairs. Ask for one or two volunteers to tell their stories to the whole group. Say: "Experiences when we temporarily lose our sight can be frightening; they make us grateful for the ability to see. It's difficult to imagine someone willingly giving up the ability to see clearly. Codependents protect themselves from reality by choosing a kind of blindness. You've studied it this week, and we'll share our thoughts from our study during this session."

Ask the group to turn to page 32 in the member's book and look at the box, "Why they deny reality." Emphasize again the truth of the third statement and the statement beginning "Remember:" after the bullets on page 33 of the member's book.

5. Pray together, asking God to supply the courage to be honest in each other's presence and thanking Him for His presence.

Group Sharing Time (30 minutes)

1. Ask the group members to divide into six teams as equal in number as possible. (One person can be a team.) Assign each team one of the defense tactics described on

pages 34-37 of the member's book. For tactic #3, give one team the subject "Extremes" described in the first four paragraphs and another team "Exaggerations" described in the last two paragraphs. Ask teams to review the material for each tactic and to find the key phrase or sentence that best summarizes and describes that tactic.

Allow five minutes for this review and discussion. Then ask for everyone's attention. Listen to each team's report.

Review the group's understanding of these defense tactics by sharing answers to the exercise concerning Helen's story at the top of page 38 of the member's book.

2. Offer a three-minute summary of the role of "blinders" in a codependent's lack of objectivity. Refer to the clippings group members attached to the poster board or bulletin board when they entered. The clippings were examples of "blinders" behavior.

Invite group members to turn to page 43 of the member's book and read what they wrote in the first exercise about the function and effect of blinders. Discuss together insights and questions.

Finally remind group members of the prayer exercise on page 43 of the member's book. Ask for prayer testimonies from that experience.

3. Invite group members to find a partner. When everyone is settled, ask partners to share the thoughts they wrote in the blank and the margin box at the top of page 44 of the member's book.

Conclude by asking a volunteer willing to share a step he plans to take to remove one of the blinders in his life. Read aloud the summary statements on page 44 of the member's book.

Small-Group Sharing Time (20 minutes)

1. For small-group sharing time ask members to keep their partners from the previous activity.

Remind the group members they will be practicing objectivity skills throughout the course. Remind them that doing so early in their study will help them build and strengthen this skill during the weeks ahead. Further, affirm the group members for practicing objectivity in days 4 and 5 on a potentially difficult subject area—relationships with parents and with God.

2. Invite partners to turn to page 47 of the member's book, and ask them to describe to each other how they felt after doing the two inventories and why they felt that way. (Ask them to base their remarks on answers in the left margin box.)

Ask group members to reflect on the prayer experience which ended day 4 and to explain to their partners any insight they gained.

Invite group members to share and discuss together the week's memory verse, Isaiah 42:16. Ask them to complete the sentence, "When I think of God's promise to guide me and to prepare the way for me, I feel …"

Closure (20 minutes)

1. Ask group members to pull out the envelope with the extra writing assignments the member's book asked them to do on page 51. Say: "On those two sheets of paper you summarized a great deal of introspection about your understanding of God based on your understanding of your parents or caregivers. Reread what you wrote this week; at the bottom of each page, write out a prayer to God. Say to Him whatever you need to say at this moment. Be honest about your joy, your confusion, your pain, your anger, your needs. I'll give you 10 minutes to write.

"If you finish before 10 minutes are up and would like to ask me or (apprentice's name) to read or discuss what you've written, please feel free to call on us."

2. Call time after 10 minutes. Ask group members to put their papers back in the envelopes, seal them, and address them to themselves. Collect the envelopes; inform the group they will receive these in the mail before unit 6.

3. Stand in a circle with hands joined. Invite any member willing to complete the following statement:

"God, for so long I've felt you were _____ , but I want to know You as _____ ." Affirm the courage of each one who shares, and with everyone's eyes open, pray a sentence prayer asking for God's guidance and encouragement for each person who speaks. Close by praying for remaining group members.

After the Session

❑ At the beginning of unit 6 in this leader's guide, place the envelopes you collected during this session.
❑ Make a copy of the leader worksheet, "Evaluating Each Session." Use this to assess the second session. If you have an apprentice, complete and discuss this worksheet with him or her.
❑ Read "Before the Session" for Group Session 3 (on the following page) to evaluate the amount of preparation

required for your next group session. Record at the top of the Group Session 3 material when you will do your preparation.
❑ Carefully study unit 3 and do all the exercises in the member's book.
❑ Pray for each group member specifically before the next group session. Especially pray for group members with special needs.
❑ Call each group member; encourage her in her study of unit 3; thank him for his commitment to the group.

Group Session 3

A Warped Sense of Responsibility

Session Goals

This session is designed to help members—
recognize unhealthy expressions of responsibility in families;
explore the "savior complex" and "Judas complex" as two ways of better understanding unhealthy responsibility;
ask for group support as they begin to practice a more healthy form of responsibility.

Before the Session

❑ Read and complete the learning activities for unit 3 in *Untangling Relationships* member's book.
❑ Find a quiet time and place to pray for group members by name. Ask the Lord to give you the wisdom you need to prepare for and lead the group session.
❑ Read the "During the Session" section which follows. Select the activities that best suit your group members' learning needs.
❑ Decide on the amount of time you want to allow for each activity. Note these times in the margin of your leader's guide as a reminder during the group time.
❑ Arrange the chairs in a circle.
❑ Make enough copies of Worksheet 2 for the group to use during the introductory activity.
❑ Gather four blank sheets of newsprint. Tape them to a focal wall. Gather markers.
❑ Arrange for a photocopier to be available during the time group members are arriving.

During the Session

Introductory Activity (25 minutes)

1. Welcome group members as they arrive. Give each a copy of Worksheet 2. Ask group members to begin working on it. Ask them to hand you their member's books opened to page 60, and assure them no one without their permission will be reading anything they've written. Send the apprentice with the opened books to the photocopier; ask him to copy page 60 and insert into each member's book the copy as he makes it; and ask him to close each book, taking care not to read what members wrote.

2. At the time to begin the session, ask for everyone's attention. Say: "This unit may have been the most personal one yet. All of us have struggled with a feeling of responsibility for others or for situations."

Ask a volunteer to stand by each piece of blank newsprint taped to the focal wall. Give each volunteer a marker. Ask group members who are willing to share what they've written to call out answers for statement 1 on the worksheet; ask one volunteer to record answers as members give them. Proceed with each statement on the worksheet as volunteers record answers on the blank sheets.

Many of the answers will be humorous; do not miss opportunities to laugh together, especially when the one giving the answer is laughing. Affirm the benefits of discovering the funny side of life. Some answers may be difficult to share; encourage those who are willing to share but who are struggling to do so.

Thank your volunteers.

3. Say: "This unit about a warped sense of responsibility begins with exercises concerning persons in your immediate or extended family. What is the link between family and a personal trait like being overly responsible or irresponsible?"

Moderate the group discussion. Then point members to the day 1 summary statements on page 55 of the member's book. Emphasize how dysfunctional families produce both kinds of warped responsibility in their members in order to maintain some sense of balance or normalcy.

4. Invite group members to read responses they wrote to the exercise on page 55. Remind them that honestly identifying a pattern repeated in their families is an important first step in choosing whether to keep the pattern or replace it with a more healthy one.

Pause and pray that the group members throughout the remainder of the group session will have the same courage they displayed.

Discovery-Group Sharing Mime (30 minutes)

1. Offer a five-minute mini lecture summarizing the day 2 material in the member's book. Ask group members to turn to page 58 of the member's book. As you read the statements from the last exercise on the page, encourage

group members to read their rewritten statements. Discuss: "On a scale of 1 to 10, with 1 being extremely easy and 10 being extremely difficult, how difficult was it for you to think differently than those original statements and to rewrite them?"

2. **Divide** the group into two groups with one being the Savior group and the other being the Judas group. Say: "You may have reacted very strongly to the day 3 and day 4 material. Identifying savior-like behavior and/or Judas-like behavior is very important to emotional and spiritual health. The extremes of responsibility are clear indicators of codependency. This material is very important to help us understand a warped sense of responsibility."

Assign each group to reread "One Family's Story" on page 53 of the member's book and as they read to find examples of savior or Judas behaviors or words. After a few minutes, invite the groups to summarize their findings. Engage the large group in a discussion of the family patterns in the story which resulted in savior or Judas behaviors and words.

Invite those who are willing to do so to contribute their story anonymously from page 60 of the member's book to hand it to you face up. Ask those who prefer not to contribute to hand the copy to you face down. Ask the two groups to regather. Give half of the face-up stories to each group. Ask them to read one or two and decide if savior or Judas behaviors and words are present. After a few moments call again for reports and discussion.

Small-Group Sharing Time (20 minutes)

1. **Invite** group members to find a partner from among their small group members. Ask partners to turn to page 62 of the member's book and to share answers to the first two written exercises. ("When do you feel like a savior/Judas? How do you act?")

Then ask them to discuss with each other answers to the written exercise on page 64 of the member's book.

("Which of the three patterns above best describes your life and experience?") Finally, invite them to review their written responses beginning on the bottom of page 66 using the question, "How does this affect others and their lives?" on page 67.

2. **Ask** partners to review the memory verses for unit 3.

Closure (15 minutes)

1. Call members back to the large group. Tell members you're not asking them to divulge details of their discussion with partners but that you are asking for members who are willing to share the two positive thoughts or actions they wrote at the bottom of page 67 of the member's book. Encourage those who offer their reflections.

2. Ask for members who are willing to share the key statement they recorded on page 68 in the unit review.

3. Briefly preview unit 4.

4. Just before the group dismisses, ask partners to pair up for prayer time. Ask partners to voice prayers for each other.

After the Session

❏ Pray for each group member specifically before the next group session, especially praying for group members with special needs.
❏ Make a copy of the leader worksheet, "Evaluating Each Session." Use this to assess the third session. If you have an apprentice, complete and discuss this worksheet with him or her.
❏ Call group members; encourage them in their study of unit 4; thank them for their commitment to the group.
❏ Read "Before the Session" for Group Session 4 to evaluate the amount of preparation required for your next group session. Record at the top of the Group Session 4 material when you will do your preparation.
❏ Study carefully unit 4 and do all the exercises in the member's book.

Group Session 4

Controlled/Controlling

Session Goals

This session is designed to help members—
honestly assess how important control is in their behavior toward others and in others' relationships with them;
share personal stories and insights with a partner and with the group;
through memory verse activities clearly choose the lordship of Christ in their lives over any other control.

Before the Session

❑ Read and complete the learning activities for unit 4 in *Untangling Relationships* member's book.
❑ Find a quiet time and place to pray for group members by name. Ask the Lord to give you the wisdom you need to prepare for and lead the group session.
❑ Write the word control vertically in large letters on a chalkboard or piece of newsprint. Be sure the word you have written is easily accessible to group members as they enter the room.
❑ On a piece of brightly colored paper, write these instructions: "Think of words to describe control or that are synonyms of control. These words may have positive connotations or negative connotations. Use the letters of the word *control* to record your ideas. Your words may begin or end with the letters of the word *control*, or use the letters in *control* in the middle of your words." Post these instructions prominently beside the chalkboard or newsprint.
❑ Gather enough three-by-five-inch cards for each group member to have one.
❑ Make copies of Worksheet 3.

During the Session

Introductory Activity (15 minutes)

1. As group members enter the room, invite them to write several responses to the activity on the chalkboard or newsprint.

Debrief the opening exercise. Read each word that members wrote on the newsprint. Stop and ask members to clarify as needed. Ask the group members to discuss which words they listed have positive connotations and which have negative connotations. Listen carefully; the group members may consider as positive some negative, or unhealthy, traits that they have used to describe control. Be ready to point out some of the difficulties of discussing control; for example, we tend to admire people who are "all together," who know how to get things done, and how to get people moving. In discussing control we can distinguish this kind of healthy, productive controlling from unhealthy controlling such as the manipulation of people's lives that unit 4 in the member's book discusses.

2. Ask for any members willing to do so to share the key statement they recorded in the unit review in the member's book. Use these statements as an overview of the unit.

Small-Group Sharing Time (25 minutes)

1. Say: "The day 1 material in the member's book opened with the statement: 'Codependents are easily controlled.' As you studied, you became aware of how true this statement is. Day 1's material mentions two primary ways codependents are vulnerable to being manipulated or controlled. What are they?" (motivation by guilt; motivation by comparison).

2. Instruct group members to find partners and turn to the chart on page 72 of the member's book. Ask them to share with each other the chart answers they wrote describing situations in which they felt manipulated by guilt and manipulated by comparison. Caution them not to share the information containing names or identifying details they wrote in the first two rows of boxes in the chart but to stick to information they wrote in the last three rows of boxes in the chart. These last three rows of boxes ask them questions about how they felt and how they responded.
After partners have had time to share, ask for volunteers to share with the group some their answers to the "motivation by guilt" questions on the chart. Discuss written responses to the exercise on the bottom of page 71 of the member's book.

Then ask for volunteers to share with the group some of their answers on the "motivation by comparison" questions on the chart. Discuss answers recorded to the first written exercise on page 72 of the member's book.

Group Sharing Time (30 minutes)

1. Ask members to turn to the top of page 73 of the member's book and to circle or highlight the boxed material. Emphasize again that manipulation is not a harmless game but is a dangerous one which perpetuates dysfunction and codependency.

2. Examine answers members wrote in the left margin box on page 75 of the member's book about how it feels to get caught in manipulation games. Encourage group members to be very honest about these feelings. Honesty is very important here because group members may hesitate for others to hear them disclose the fact that they have had feelings like fear or shame.

Distribute the three-by-five-inch cards. Ask group members to write on the cards one example of manipulation they've used on another person which is similar to the kind of manipulation others have used on them.

Then ask them to list an example of manipulation they've used on another person which is *different* than the manipulation others have used on them.

(You may provide a few personal examples or refer to some illustrations in the unit 4 material to help group members complete this exercise.)

Now, refer back to the definitions of codependency on pages 22-23 of unit 1 in the member's book. Ask: "Do you find that any of these descriptions of codependency fit the manipulative behaviors you have just listed? Is someone willing to tell the group any insights he or she has just experienced from this exercise?" Empathetically process the group discussion that follows. Affirm those who share painful personal insights. Remind the group that the value of identifying patterns of behavior is the first step toward intentionally choosing how we will act and think.

Closure (20 minutes)

1. Ask group members to return to the partners they had during the small-group sharing time. Instruct partners to tell each other about the activity from day 2 of the member's book which asked them to tape three-by-five-inch cards to various items that represented areas they carefully control in their lives. Ask partners to reveal to each other a list of items to which they taped the cards or to tell how they chose the items on which to tape them. Explain that the items chosen might represent particular persons in their lives.

When partners complete this sharing, ask the group to call out items to which cards were taped. As you hear each answer, instruct group members to say the memory verse and to personalize the verse by using one of the items mentioned in the preface. For example, they will state: "(*Item or person mentioned*) does not control us. 'For the love of Christ controls us, having concluded this, that one died for all, therefore all died; Therefore if any man is in Christ, he is a new creature; the old things passed away; behold, new things have come.' " This activity may take several minutes to complete as group members offer their answers; do not rush the activity.

2. Distribute Worksheet 3. Allow five minutes for work. Call time; commit to the Lord in prayer all that's been said and done, especially during the closure time. Before you offer the prayer, allow anyone willing to share with the group a specific concern about control issues in his or her life.

3. Preview unit 5. Alert group members to the fact that day 5 includes a lengthy inventory which will require extra time to work through and to process.

After the Session

❑ Remember, this unit asks group members honestly to face abuse in their lives. It asks them to do this whether they are being abused (see page 75 of the member's book) or are abusive (see page 83 of the member's book). Be prepared that some members may request your help or referral to deal with some aspect of abuse.

❑ Make a copy of Leader Worksheet, "Evaluating Each Session." Use this to assess the fourth session. If you have an apprentice, complete and discuss this worksheet with him or her.

❑ Read "Before the Session" for Group Session 5 (on the following page) to evaluate the amount of preparation required for your next group session. Record at the top of the Group Session 5 material when you will do your preparation.

❑ Carefully study unit 5 and do all the exercises in the member's book.

Group Session 5

Hurt and Anger

Session Goals

This session is designed to help members—
recognize abuse in their lives-both abuse from others toward them and abuse they heap on themselves;
thoroughly understand the six responses codependents make to hurt and anger;
evaluate any evidences of these six responses in their own lives;
face the possibility of peeling back protective layers and of honestly facing past and present wounds.

Before the Session

❑ Read and complete the learning activities for unit 5 in *Untangling Relationships* member's book.
❑ Find a quiet time and place to pray for group members by name. Ask the Lord to give you the wisdom you need to prepare for and lead the group session.
❑ Prepare six sentence strips. On each one of them print one of the following responses to hurt and anger: numbness; pain without gain; excusing the offender/ blaming themselves; displaced anger; outbursts of anger; and using self-pity and anger to manipulate others.
❑ Make enough copies of Worksheet 4 for half of your group; do the same with copies of Worksheet 5.
❑ Use a large sheet of newsprint or poster board to make four arrows. Use the same large sheet of newsprint or poster board to make the following signs: excusing the offender; blaming ourselves; feeling the offender's guilt; confessing the offender's sin.
❑ Purchase enough onions for everyone in the group to have one. Bring a roll of paper towels.

Remember that these activities are to assist you as you lead the group. Your group may desire and need to use a more simple format in which group members simply share how the study is impacting their lives. Your prayer and preparation will free you to assist the group process with learning activities as needed.

During the Session

Introductory Activity (15 minutes)

1. Warmly greet group members as they arrive. Ask them to find the cartoon response they added on page 90 of the member's book and share it with at least three other group members before the group begins.

Begin the group. Remark that the cartoon ending to Marianne and Kyle's story perfectly illustrates the primary need of codependents—to change hurtful, abusive, or codependent patterns of relating to others.

2. Direct group members' attention to the definition of abuse on page 88 of the member's book. Ask them to highlight or circle the definition's three key verbs—*control, subjugate,* and *wear down*—as a summary of the methods and effects of abuse. Tell members that the presence of these words in the definition indicate why hurt and anger occur so easily in codependent relationships. Ask members to highlight or circle the first paragraph under "Hurt and Anger" on page 89 of the member's book.

Lead the group in a few moments of silent prayer. Instruct the group to contrast the unit memory verses, Hebrews 4:15-16 with the paragraph on hurt and anger, which they just read. Close the time of silent prayer with a prayer of thanksgiving for Jesus—our great High Priest.

Discovery-Group Sharing Time (35 minutes)

1. Give half the group Worksheet 4 and half the group Worksheet 5. Ask group members to read instructions and work individually and silently.

Then ask members of the two groups to gather and to share answers from their worksheets. Appoint one scribe in each group; provide each scribe with a clean copy of his or her group's worksheet. Compile the most insightful answers.

Call time after 10 minutes, and ask group members to give reports on the compilations. Preface each report by giving the page number in the member's book of the story from the unit to which the worksheets refer.

2. Say: "On days 2 through 4 in the member's book you studied six ways codependents respond to hurt and anger. Look on page 91 of the member's book at the sentences after the two bullets. (Call on one group member to read these statements aloud.) In just a moment we will discuss these six behaviors. As we do we will study how well we understand each response and how well we can apply each response to our lives."

Lead a discussion of these six behaviors. Post the sentence strip listing each behavior as it is mentioned. In the discussion listen for group members' *understanding* of each behavior.

As you finish discussing each behavior, ask group members to apply each behavior to their own lives. After you discuss each behavior, ask: "Do you typically respond to hurt and anger in this way?" You may want to encourage group members to share by giving them time to explore their feelings regarding anger or by telling their own stories.

Illustrate the third behavior, "excusing the offender/blaming themselves" by enlisting four volunteers to hold the four signs you made. Ask volunteers to stand in the order excusing the offender, blaming ourselves, feeling the offender's guilt, and confessing the offender's sin.

Use the last two paragraphs of page 96 of the member's book to explain this cycle. As you explain each of the four signs, give an arrow to the volunteer holding the sign you're explaining. Ask the volunteer to use the arrow to point to the next sign.

Conclude your explanation by asking volunteers to move from standing in a straight line to standing in a circle. Explain that this illustrates the cyclical nature of this response.

Conclude the discussion of the six responses by asking group members to highlight or circle the second definition of abuse—self abuse—contained in the boxed material near the bottom of page 93 of the member's book.

Tell the group members that people often see this self-abuse response occurring because codependents repeat the patterns of behavior directed against them—if not against another person, then against themselves. Members may desire and need to spend time sharing how self-abuse patterns have affected their lives.

Small-Group Sharing Time (25 minutes)

1. Ask group members to gather in groups of three. Ask them to spend their first few moments reviewing the memory passage. When they finish reviewing it, explain that Jesus had the choice to respond to the hurt and anger in His life in the same improper ways that we do. Even though He did not respond improperly, He faced the same choices about His behavior that we face. Challenge group members to use this truth to help them be honest in the sharing time.

2. Ask small-group members to share what they've written in response to the first exercise on page 101 of the member's book and in response to the answers to "Reflection" on pages 105-106 of the member's book. Allow sufficient time for all members to share.

Closure (15 minutes)

1. Ask the group members to stand in a circle, and give each member an onion. Remind them this unit began with a picture of an onion cut in half (see page 91 of the member's book). The picture of the cut onion was a tool for comparing the responses codependents make to their deep wounds to the layers and layers protecting the core of the onion.

Ask group members to use their onions to symbolize their willingness to face past deep wounds and to deal with present deep wounds honestly. Ask them to begin to peel the onions they hold. As the group members are peeling onions, ask them:

> What emotions are you feeling as you peel this onion? What insights are you having about peeling onions? What application can you make to a codependent's need to peel back the protective layers covering her hurt and anger? What might she feel? What might she find?

2. While indicating to group members that time is coming to a close, allow a moment for them to put down onions and to wipe their hands. Recite the memory passage once again. Close in a prayer for courage to peel away the protective layers of life and to learn to deal with the deep wounds of life.

After the Session

❏ Make a copy of Leader Worksheet, "Evaluating Each Session." Use this to assess the fifth session. If you have an apprentice, complete and discuss this worksheet with him or her.
❏ Read "Before the Session" for Group Session 6.
❏ Study carefully unit 6, and do all the exercises in the member's book.
❏ Unit 6 provides an explanation of how to become a Christian. Be especially prayerful for any non-Christian in your group as he or she encounters this information. You may want to meet with any nonChristians individually before the next group session; offer to answer any questions they have about becoming a Christian and relate your testimony to them.
❏ Mail the envelopes collected at the end of Group Session 2 to group members; be sure the envelopes arrive before your time scheduled for Group Session 6.

Group Session 6

Guilt and Shame

Session Goals

This session is designed to help members—
clearly separate codependent guilt which leads to shame from the objective guilt God uses to bring confession and forgiveness;
describe the effects of guilt in their lives;
study Scriptures explaining their identity in Christ;
share personal decisions they have made and celebrate decisions others have made to become Christians or to settle some of the control issues in their lives.

Before the Session

❏ Read and complete the learning activities for unit 6 in *Untangling Relationships* member's book.
❏ Find a quiet time and place to pray for group members by name. Ask the Lord to give you the wisdom you need to prepare for and lead the group session.
❏ Read the "During the Session" section which follows. Select the activities that best suit your group members' learning needs.
Unit 6 deals with crucial issues—guilt and shame. During this study some group members likely will confront the dysfunction in their relationships. If you have any options with time, consider a slightly longer format for this session. Do not rush through the material or the group members' reactions to it.
❏ Decide on the amount of time you want to allow for each activity. Note these times in the margin of your leader's guide as a reminder during group time. Always be prepared to change your plans as the Holy Spirit leads you and as the needs of the group or an individual dictate.
❏ Arrange the chairs in a circle.
❏ Secure a choir robe and a bowl of mints. just outside the meeting room place a table with a chair behind it. On the table place the bowl containing the mints.
❏ Make enough copies of Worksheet 6 so that one is available for each group member.
❏ Acquire six large poster boards or pieces of newsprint and prepare the following placards:
I only see the pressure of it in my peripheral vision.
I occasionally bump against one side or the other of the pressure.
I feel a constant, steady pressure from it but manage to go on in spite of it.
The pressure fluctuates wildly; some days I'm not aware of it, and other days I hardly can breathe because of it.
The pressure never lets up.
I feel like the life is being crushed out of me.
Make enough copies of Worksheet 7 for each group member to have one worksheet.

During the Session

(Note: Even with the best of planning, this session likely cannot be processed effectively in 90 minutes. Attempt to allow more time for this session. (You may choose to study this unit for two sessions, to conduct a two-hour session; or to devise some other plan which provides additional time.)

Introductory Activity (20 minutes)

1. Dress your apprentice in the choir robe you brought and seat him or her behind the table. As group members arrive, the apprentice will say: "I am the judge, and (holding out a mint) this is my judgment. Will you accept it?" If the individual says yes, the judge hands him or her the mint and says, "My judgment is that you bravely have embarked on an important journey. You may enter this room and rest." If a group member says no, the judge says, "My judgment is that you are fearful of the journey ahead. Rest here a moment, and then try again in a moment to accept my judgment."

Ask whether the group members felt restful studying unit 6 and whether they feel restful about tonight's session. Invite them to talk freely about how they felt as they studied this unit about guilt and shame.

2. Call group members to the circle; remind them that day 1 began with the title, "Never Good Enough." Ask:
How are you never good enough?
When are you never good enough?
Why are you never good enough?

Stress that the guilt codependents feel about not being good enough produces shame and destroys their lives. The guilt God sends does not do this. Review the differences in codependent guilt and objective guilt. As a guide use the chart on page 110 in the member's book.

Small-Group Sharing Time (15 minutes)

1. Ask group members to find partners and discuss how the mail they received (activity completed in unit 2 and Group Session 2) affected the study of guilt and shame in this unit. Ask partners to discuss how a better understanding of who God is helps us deal with our guilt. After a few moments, ask several group members to share their insights with the entire group.

2. Give group members copies of "Emma's Dilemma" from Worksheet 6. Allow two minutes to complete it. Then ask them to form two groups. Allow the two groups five minutes to stage a debate. One group will try to convince the others that Emma, when she grows to adulthood, will be a duplicate of her parents. The other group will try to convince the others that Emma in adulthood will be the opposite of her parents. Allow both groups time to plan their speeches. Call time and hear reports. Use the debate to reinforce the fact that codependent patterns are pervasive throughout families.

Discovery-Group Sharing Time (1 hour)

1. Review the origin of the term *codependency* (it originated with those treating addicted persons; it first emerged in the world of addiction). Refer to the first paragraph under "The Grip of Addiction" on page 121 in the member's book. Ask members to highlight or circle the first and last sentences of that paragraph. Emphasize and assure group members that this paragraph does not tell a truth to affix blame but tells a truth to affirm our personal choice. Ask group members to remember the doctor's words quoted on page 122 in their member's books, "Your addiction is not your fault; your response to it is."

2. Lead a discussion about the impact of guilt in persons' lives. Look first at the vise pictured on page 118 in the member's book. Point out the placards posted around the room. Ask each group member to look again at the vise illustration and imagine that he or she is the person in the middle of the vise. Ask: "Which of these phrases on the wall best describes you and how you felt about guilt before you began this group?" Ask group members to stand beside the placard that represents the most appropriate answer for them. Allow group members to share the meaning of their choices.

Then ask: "Which phrase best describes you and how you felt about guilt today after you studied this unit? Stand by the phrase that best describes your answer." Be sensitive to some group members who indicate that they feel more burdened by guilt today than they did before they began this course. Affirm the fact that they're being honest, and assure them that peeling back layers over deep wounds often brings more pain before the healing begins.

3. Ask group members to return to the circle. Encourage volunteers to share their responses to the first written exercise (about turning the guilt handle on yourself) on page 118 in the member's book. Then ask: "Based on your study of day 1 in this unit, is guilt ever a positive experience?" Carefully direct this discussion. Even objective guilt which leads us to confession and forgiveness begins with facing inadequacies, failures, or sins, and these are painful, but productive, moments in anyone's life.

Turn to Keith's story on pages 121-122 in the member's book. Take time to read it aloud. Ask for responses group members recorded in the exercise which follows the story. Candidly discuss feelings, especially as group members personalize this story and apply it to their own feelings.

Conclude by reading the paragraph labeled "Attitude of Selfishness" and found on page 122 in the member's book. Remind group members that selfishness (choosing my own way over God's way) prevents non-Christians from accepting God's gift of salvation and hinders Christians from daily knowing God's forgiveness and grace. Tell members, "Codependency is one expression of our self-centeredness."

4. Distribute Worksheet 7. Ask group members to work individually. Share answers by designating one person to read the fill-in-the-blank portion of the exercise until he or she reaches the first blank; then ask the person on his or her left to pick up reading until he or she reaches the next blank, and so on until members read aloud all the paragraphs.

Say: "These Scriptures summarize your identity in Christ. On day 4 you read to three people a beautiful affirmation of this identity. The affirmation is found on page 120 in your member's book. Find a partner among group members. Read this affirmation to your partner. Let your partner read it to you. Then pray together a prayer of thanksgiving for the identity God offers you in Christ."

Closure (25 minutes)

1. As you observe most partners finishing their final prayer activity, sing softly a praise chorus that you know will be familiar to your group. Gesture for partners who are finished to stand by you as you form a circle.

Encourage them to join you in softly singing the praise song. Continue to play or sing until everyone rejoins the

circle and joins hands.
Acknowledge the eternal significance of what you've studied this week and processed in the group session. Provide time for anyone who needs to share a personal insight or prayer request.

Again, be sensitive; someone in your group may be a new Christian, and the group needs to celebrate this fact. Some Christians may have made significant decisions about control in their lives, and the group needs to celebrate this.

As each person concludes his or her prayer, you as leader can pray a sentence prayer for each person who has shared and for his or her specific need or situation. Wrap up this sharing time by praying for any others in the group who may not have shared and who you have not yet mentioned by name in prayer.

2. Briefly preview unit 7. Explain that this is a difficult unit, too, but it is an important one to study before they begin the process of understanding recovery in unit 8.

3. Ask group members to recite the unit memory passages and to call out the positive promises they hold. Affirm God's power to release us from fear, guilt, and shame. Close by repeating the passage again; play or sing the praise chorus as members depart.

After the Session

❏ If any group member made a significant decision during this unit's study, schedule individual appointments with him or her. These appointments may be for encouragement, to answer questions, and to support the decision the person has made.
❏ Make a copy of Leader Worksheet, "Evaluating Each Session." Use this to assess the sixth session. If you have an apprentice, complete and discuss this worksheet with him or her.
❏ Read "Before the Session" for Group Session 7 to evaluate the amount of preparation required for your next group session. Record at the top of the Group Session 7 material a time when you will do your preparation.
❏ Study carefully unit 7 and do all the exercises in the member's book.

Group Session 7

Lonely and Pressured

Session Goals

This session is designed to help members—
- simulate in a safe environment the pain of loneliness;
- assess the consequences of loneliness in a codependent's life with the group's help;
- evaluate ways codependency mars relationships with God and views of the Scriptures;
- honestly confront one attitude or behavior which separates them from others or from God.

Before the Session

- ❏ Read and complete the learning activities for unit 7 in *Untangling Relationships* member's book.
- ❏ Find a quiet time and place to pray for group members by name. Ask the Lord to give you the wisdom you need to prepare for and lead the group session.
- ❏ Arrange the chairs in a circle. Enlarge the circle with maximum space between chairs; then turn the chairs so they face outside rather than inside the circle.
- ❏ Obtain a roll of aluminum foil and tear off enough large squares to give one to each group member.
- ❏ On a large sheet of newsprint, print the following statements. Keep the newsprint rolled up or out of sight until the closure activity.
  - One thing I use to keep me separated from others is...
  - One thing I use to keep me separated from God is...
  - One thing I've learned about myself and my loneliness is..

Remember that these activities are to assist you as you lead the group. Your group may desire and need to use a more simple format in which group members simply share how the study is impacting their lives. Your prayer and preparation will free you to assist the group process with learning activities as needed.

During the Session

Introductory Activity (10 minutes)

1. Play quiet, reflective music as group members enter. Greet members, and in a low tone of voice, ask them to select chairs, open their member's book to page 125, and begin reviewing the day 1 material.

2. After all members have arrived and completed the assignment, interrupt them and begin processing this experience. Discuss how they felt about their assignment. Say: "In a room full of people, you may have had the experience of feeling 'lonely in a crowd.' " Affirm the common experience of loneliness which codependents have as a way to connect with others having the same experience. Even a painful experience like loneliness provides a touchpoint for codependents to understand and reach out to each other.

Discovery-Group Sharing Time (45 minutes)

1. Invite group members to turn their chairs to face the inside of the circle and to pull chairs in and tighten up the circle. Say: "Codependents, who feel lonely struggle in some key areas—feeling abandoned by people and feeling abandoned by God. Sometimes they cannot genuinely begin to restore their relationship to God until they are able to restore relationships with people. You may feel some of these same feelings. But we are halfway through an experience together in which we've been honest in one another's presence. The fact that we are here tonight affirms that we have not abandoned each other.

"We will take a few minutes now to symbolize both our loneliness and our desire to be more honest with ourselves and with others."

Give each group member a large square of foil. Instruct them to press it against their faces. Ask them to use their fingers and carefully mold their facial features into the foil. Remind them to include the sides of their faces and the area under the chin. As members begin to finish the task, ask them to keep the foil in front of their faces. (Once the molding is finished, members may prefer to hold the mask loosely in front of their faces for ease in breathing! The goal is to keep their vision blocked for the next few moments.) Ask: "What is it like to live behind a mask?" (Answers may run the gamut from "lonely" to "safe." Accept and affirm insights given.)

While members still have their masks in place, read aloud the paragraph labeled "Hiding from love" found on page 130 in the member's book. Also read to the members the bullet statements which follow the paragraph. Then ask: "I'm wondering if anyone is willing to confess before this group just what I've been reading. I'm wondering whether anyone feels he or she has ever put up false fronts, been afraid of risking closeness, built facades, or lied. If you feel that you have, please lower your mask and share your thoughts with the group."

When sharing begins to slow, affirm the courage of those who contributed, and ask all group members to take their masks down and to affix these masks to the wall or a bulletin board, being careful not to disturb the masks' shape. Ask group members to stand and look at the masks and describe to the group what they see. (You may hear answers like "a face frozen," "closed, unseeing eyes," or "vulnerability—the aluminum can be crushed easily.") Then ask what insights group members have gained about living behind masks. When sharing concludes, ask group members to return to the circle of chairs.

2. Remind group members that you began by talking about the abandonment codependents often feel. Another expression of this feeling is that codependents often feel abandoned by authority. Remind them they read about this in day 2 material in the member's book. Review the group's identification with this concept. Do this by asking volunteers to share how they responded to the margin box on page 129 in the member's book.

Say: "This group has become like an authority in your individual lives. You've testified to, and I've observed the fact that you've accepted insights from each other you initially resisted or rejected in written form in the book. You've shared a great deal of life together through this group experience, and you've invested in the group a degree of credibility and authority you do not give to the written word in your member's book. And that is OK to do—it is one of the greatest advantages of a group experience. In a group experience like this, words, concepts, and thoughts begin to live and breathe and take on meaning.

"But my question is this: Have you had an experience of feeling toward the group what you just indicated you felt toward authority as you shared your responses that you wrote in the margin box?"

Encourage group members to share their attitudes toward authority and toward the group as an expression of authority.

3. Highlight the definition of *grace* found on page 132 in the member's book. Take time to discuss members' responses to the review activity on the same page. Ask a volunteer to read aloud the last paragraph on page 133. Ask group members to volunteer answers to the question in the last sentence of that paragraph.

Small-Group Sharing Time (20 minutes)

1. Ask group members to find a partner—if possible, someone they've not partnered with yet. Ask partners to turn to page 134 in their member's book to review the information about misinterpreting the Scriptures, and to tell how they responded to the first written exercise on the page.

2. Ask partners to turn to page 137 in their member's book and to discuss the memory work questions they find in the paragraph marked by the boldface arrow.

3. Conclude the time of sharing with partners by asking the partners to say the unit memory passage to each other.

Closure (15 minutes)

1. Briefly preview unit 8. Encourage group members to remain faithful to their study and to their memory work.

2. Instruct group members to remove their masks from the bulletin board or wall and to bring the masks to the circle. As group members hold their masks (but not in a way to block them from each other), display the poster with the open-ended statements you prepared before the session. Ask group members to finish the statements. As each finishes, quietly instruct him or her to wad up the aluminum and toss it into the center of the circle. Then, ask a volunteer from the group to pray for the person who has just shared and for the specific need he or she mentioned. Continue this until each person has finished a statement and has been prayed for by need and by name.

3. Dismiss the group by singing the refrain of the hymn printed on page 133 of the member's book.

After the Session

❏ Make a copy of Leader Worksheet, "Evaluating Each Session." Use this to assess the seventh session. If you have an apprentice, complete and discuss this worksheet with him or her.
❏ Read "Before the Session" for Group Session 8 to evaluate the amount of preparation required for your next group session. Record at the top of the Group Session 8 material the time when you will do your preparation.
❏ Study carefully unit 8 and do all the exercises in the member's book.

Group Session 8

Identity: A Sense of Worth

Session Goals

This session is designed to help members—
answer with biblical truth the question "Who am I?";
understand how the six characteristics of codependency affect identity and damage self-worth;
learn from insights offered by the rest of the group about how God communicates to us our worth and our identity.

Before the Session

❑ Since you now are in your eighth session, members no doubt are beginning to bond with and trust each other. As a result you may find you are using the suggested content-focused activities less and less and that you needing more time for the group members to share personal insights and feelings and to hear group response to sharing. Plan to discuss the aspect of flexibility with your apprentice weekly. You even may want to negotiate this with your group. Be prayerful and sensitive about how you structure the next five group sessions. The content will lead the group members to the point of choosing change as the course concludes. The group members need to help each other reach this significant decision. As I write this I am praying God will guide you as you seek to balance learning activities versus spontaneous sharing time. When you are in doubt about which direction to go, lean toward sharing.
❑ Make three large signs to attach to a focal wall. On each sign put one of the following words: perception; love; separateness.
❑ Make two large posters; label one "Who I Am" and the other "What I Do." Affix to a focal wall that is accessible when group members enter the room. Tape several markers to the wall near each poster.
❑ Make copies of Worksheets 8 and 9. You will distribute Worksheet 9 as a take-home assignment at the end of the session.

During the Session

Introductory Activity (10 minutes)

1. As group members enter, ask them to look at responses they gave to the first three written exercises on page 144. Ask them to write on the poster labeled "Who I Am" several of the R (for roles) responses they listed; in the same way, ask them to write on the poster labeled "What I Do" several of their F (for *functions*) responses.

2. Ask everyone to come to the circle. Discuss their insights about this exercise in their books and ask whether they have compiled answers on the two posters. Be sure group members know that both roles and functions are important parts of their identities. Remind group members that unit 8 helps us strengthen our understanding of the foundation of our identity—who we are in Christ.

3. Remind group members that this unit marks the beginning of understanding recovery from codependency. Call their attention to the informal outline in the fourth paragraph on page 150 in their members' book. Recovery requires perception, love, and separateness. To highlight these important concepts in recovery use the three signs you made.

Discovery-Group Sharing Time (20 minutes)

1. Distribute Worksheet 8 to each group member. Assign one Scripture per person until all Scriptures have been assigned. Ask group members to work individually filling in their portion of the chart on the worksheet. Call time. Ask group members to stand and mingle. Ask them to swap answers and fill in their charts until you call time.

To discuss God's intent to communicate clearly who He is and what He plans for us, use the scriptural truths reflected in the chart.

Ask and discuss: "How does this knowledge make you feel about your identity?"

2. Refer group members to page 141. Ask: "What kind of change will be most significant as you accept and affirm your wonderful identity in Christ?" Ask group members to choose for their answers one of the four categories of change listed at the bottom of page 141.

Use this discussion about change to encourage those who doubt their capacity to change. Affirm those who have begun to choose change in their behaviors or beliefs as steps to recovery from codependency.

Small-Group Sharing Time (30 minutes)

1. Divide into four equal groups. Assign each group one

of the four scriptural descriptions of our identity in Christ on page 145 in the member's book. Distribute markers and large sheets of paper to each group.

Ask each group to reread the description you assigned it and then to choose an up-to-date example to illustrate it graphically. Allow several minutes for discussion and sketching. Listen to reports. Affirm the creativity in each report to clarify our identity in Christ.

2. Still working in the four groups, ask each group to discuss this question: "Why is the issue of our identity in Christ important to address?" Allow a few minutes for groups to discuss and then to report. Relate the discussions to the three primary and three secondary characteristics of codependency and to their implications for a codependent's identity.

Conclude the discussion by reviewing group members' responses made to the margin box on page 146 in their books.

3. Conclude small-group sharing time by asking group members to pair up and to share responses to the first written exercise and the margin box on page 144 in the member's book.

Remind partners to review the unit memory verse. Encourage them to share with their partners about the person they identified on day 3, page 149 in the member's book. On this page the book asked them to identify someone who needs to know the wonderful promise of this memory verse.

Closure (30 minutes)

1. Call the group members back into one group. Remind group members that unit 9 is the next logical, wonderful step from unit 8. Once we clearly understand our identity and who we are (unit 8), then finding where we belong follows naturally (unit 9).

2. Distribute Worksheet 9. Instruct group members to complete it, along with activities in unit 9, by the time they arrive at the next group session. Remind members to begin work on the worksheet in time to journal five days of entries in the third section. Briefly preview unit 9.

3. Ask group members to reunite with the partners from their small-group sharing time. Ask partners to face each other and then to form two parallel lines with partners across from each other. Then, move each line to opposite walls, putting as much distance between the two lines as your room allows. Instruct members in one line to begin making silent, physical movements which their partners

repeat and duplicate. After 15 seconds, call time and allow the second line to initiate movements. Remind partners to operate silently.

Instruct the two lines to take a giant step toward each other. Repeat the process above. Then ask the lines to move within two feet of each other and to repeat the process. Encourage partners to try to coordinate together so well that their movements are like mirror images.

Call the group back to the circle. Ask partners to sit together. Ask and discuss:

> What was the easiest part of doing this exercise?
> What was the hardest part of doing this exercise?

Say: "Now take a mental leap with me. Imagine that your partner in this exercise was Christ and that your task was to mirror His image. Take the insights you've just shared about the easiest and hardest parts of doing this exercise and apply them to your efforts to duplicate what Christ does and who He is." Help group members probe this analogy. Then read aloud the following Scriptures:

> "Therefore you are to be perfect, as your heavenly Father is perfect" (Matthew 5:48).
> "Be merciful, just as your Father is merciful" (Luke 6:36).
> "Therefore be imitators of God, as beloved children; and walk in love, just as Christ also loved you, and gave Himself up for us, an offering and a sacrifice to God as a fragrant aroma" (Ephesians 5:1-2).

Affirm how critically important understanding who we are in Christ is to recovery. We are to imitate Him.

Lead the group in a prayer of celebration for this wonderful identity and of confession for times we do not choose to imitate Christ.

After the Session

❏ Mail a copy of Worksheet 9 to anyone absent for Group Session 8.
❏ Make a copy of Leader Worksheet, "Evaluating Each Session." Use this to assess the eighth session.

Notes

[1] This activity adapted from "Warming Up: Physically and Socially," in Sharon Baack, Hal Hill, and Joe Palmer, *Adventure Recreation: An Adventure in Group Building* (Nashville: Convention Press, 1989), 30.

Group Session 9

Belonging

Session Goals

This session is designed to help members—
discuss any fears they have about the lordship of Christ in their lives;
recall daily experiences, prior to this session, in which they identify God's love;
acknowledge the affirmation and encouragement other group members have provided during this discovery-group experience;
express love to other group members.

Before the Session

❏ Read and complete the learning activities for unit 9 in *Untangling Relationships* member's book.
❏ Find a quiet time and place to pray for each group member. Ask the Lord to give you the wisdom you need to prepare for and lead the group session.
❏ Make six placards which can be taped or pinned to clothing. On each write one of the following words: Narrator; Owner; Servant; Wife; Son; Daughter.
❏ Gather enough clothespins for each group member to have one. Attach to a focal wall a piece of sturdy string at least six feet in length. Make the following placards and affix to the wall as indicated:
  Fear Without Love; put just above the left end of the string.
  Love and Respect; put just above the middle of the string.
  Love Without Respect; put just above the right end of the string.
❏ Bring a large blanket. Affix one end to a wall so that when a person standing lifts the top corner on the opposite end, this creates an opaque barrier.

During the Session

Introductory Activity (10 minutes)

1. As members gather, ask your apprentice to hold the corner of the blanket up to form the barrier. Invite group members to stand on either side of the blanket. When all members have arrived, give these instructions: "Each group needs to bunch up in a cluster of chairs several paces back from the blanket. Be sure you cannot see the other group members and that they cannot see you. In a moment, I'll ask both groups to choose silently one member to move to the blanket and sit facing it. When I say "Go!" the blanket will be dropped, and the two people facing each other will try to name the person sitting just opposite them. The first one to shout the correct name wins the other one for his or her side."

Enjoy playing the game until one group has significantly fewer persons than the other.

2. Regroup in the circle of chairs. Relate any observations you made about the game when it was in progress. (Some persons may have begun to feel competitive about it; some may have laughed too much to speak; someone watching may have shouted out of turn.) Point out that no matter what side of the blanket you were on, you belonged in the process; no one was ever "out." Relate this to the unit they've studied about belonging and about the choices people make to belong to Christ.

Group Sharing Time (40 minutes)

1. Offer a mini lecture on codependents' seven fears about the lordship of Christ. As the basis of your mini lecture use material from pages 156-158 in the member's book. Invite group members to open their books to these pages as you talk.

After you describe each fear, interrupt your minilecture by:
pointing out (or asking a volunteer to call out) a key phrase explaining this fear; for example, the phrase "He will punish them" might be a key phrase for the first fear, "God is mean" (see page 156 in the member's book). inviting one or two group members to share the responses they wrote in their member's books after each fear.

2. Ask: "Who can recall memory verses from previous units which deal with our fears?" Possible verses might include: Isaiah 42:16 (unit 2); Hebrews 4:15-16 (unit 5); Psalm 34:4-5 (unit 6); Deuteronomy 31:6 (unit 7). Any answer meaningful to the group member responding is acceptable.

3. Enlist a volunteer to read aloud Exodus 21:1-6 (cited on page 159 in the member's book) and five additional volunteers to act out the story as the first volunteer reads it. Give each volunteer one of the six placards you previously made.
NOTE: The dramatic reading of this Scripture may not

involve movement as much as it will a series of poses as members describe different situations. Allow your group members to offer their own creative input and expression. If you think best, enlist these volunteers before the session and let them talk about this activity before the session begins.

When members finish the dramatic reading, thank the volunteers. Invite group members to share their responses for the two exercises on page 159 in the member's book.

Ask: "In light of this Old Testament background, what is the significance of the fact that the New Testament writers called themselves 'bond-servants'?" (See Scriptures printed in the margins on pages 158 and 159 in the member's book.) Use this discussion to affirm the importance of our choice to acknowledge the lordship of Christ in our lives.

Ask: "According to page 160 what do we choose by default if we do not choose Christ's lordship in our lives?" (idolatry). Discuss together how group members feel about this strong word. Conclude discussion by sharing responses to the first written exercise on page 161 in the member's book.

Small-Group Sharing Time (20 minutes)

1. Ask group members to retrieve Worksheet 9 which you distributed at the last group session.

Instruct them to find partners and share responses to Sections I and III. Call time and hear examples from Section III. As members cite examples, compile a list on the chalkboard or a sheet of newsprint. Use this activity to celebrate the diversity of God's expressions of love to us.

Say: "In unit 8 we studied the importance of honest perception for codependents who want to change. Did focusing on God's love all week through this worksheet *clear   cloud* your perception of yourself? of others?" Encourage a lively discussion. Affirm the fact that a person can experience God's love and move beyond codependency.

Ask partners to conclude this sharing time by praying for each other. To do this, ask them to swap their copies of Worksheet 9 and to pray for their partners the prayer their partners wrote in Section II on the worksheet.

Closure (20 minutes)

1. Distribute one clothespin to each group member. Invite members to clip the clothespin on the string in the same place as they placed the X on the continuum on page 160 in their books. Ask members to explain why they placed the clothespin where they did. Use this activity to affirm our choice to accept God's love and His lordship.

2. Remind the group members that on day 5 they studied the need for a special kind of friend who makes the idea of belonging have flesh and blood. In another place in the unit, they studied some positive relational results that come from honesty and love. Invite group members to turn to pages 166-167 in their books. Read each bulleted paragraph out loud. Then ask: "When did you experience this in this group? Or, who in this group made this truth real to you?"

Listen carefully. Be sure that when sharing concludes group members have mentioned everyone at least once by name.

Invite group members to turn to the box on page 171 in the member's book. Ask: "Were you able to list names of people you could affirm or encourage?" Discuss whether this assignment was easy or difficult.

Remember, some of your group members still may be so needy they do not have anything to give to another yet. Such an assignment would have been difficult or even impossible for them. If they are willing to say that this was difficult or impossible, affirm their courage and honesty.

3. Close by reciting the unit memory verses together. Encourage group members to linger awhile and to express their love to one another.

After the Session

❑ Make a copy of Leader Worksheet, "Evaluating Each Session." Use this to assess the ninth session. If you have an apprentice, complete and discuss this worksheet with him or her.
❑ Read "Before the Session" for Group Session 10 (on the following page) to evaluate the amount of preparation you will need for your next group session. Record at the top of the Group Session 10 material a time when you will do your preparation.
❑ Study carefully unit 10 and do all the exercises in the member's book.

Notes

[1] This activity adapted from "Warming Up: Physically and Socially," in Sharon Baack, Hal Hill, and Joe Palmer, *Adventure Recreation: An Adventure in Group Building* (Nashville: Convention Press, 1989), 28.

Group Session 10

Three-Step Process to a Healthy Life

Session Goals

This session is designed to help members—
- clearly understand the three-step process to a healthy life;
- practice each of the three steps studied in this unit;
- commit to prayer important decisions they made in the study and in the session;
- honestly identify fears they have and benefits they anticipate in choosing a healthy life over a codependent one.

Before the Session

❑ Make three large placards: Identify; Detach; Decide. Affix placards to three walls in the meeting room. Plan to have members turn their chairs so that they face the appropriate word representing the part of the three-step process you are studying at that point in the session.
❑ Gather three or four unusual objects. Place each on a chair in a different part of the session room. Cover each object with a towel.
❑ Make copies of Worksheets 10 and 11 for group members.

During the Session

Introductory Activity (15 minutes)

1. As group members enter, direct them to the chairs displaying the towel-draped objects. Ask members to try to identify the objects without looking at the actual objects. Members may look at an object's shape while draped, they may smell it, or they may reach under the towel and touch it.

When everyone has arrived, call the group together. Use the "Identify" placard for the focal wall. Call for speculation about the hidden objects; non specific responses are unacceptable! Saying, "It's a book," is no challenge; guessing "It's *Webster's Ninth Edition Dictionary*" takes more courage! Enjoy the discussion.

Remind group members that their study of unit 10 was a study about the importance of identifying. Group members learned a three-step process for recovery from codependency. Step one in the process is identification.

2. Present a brief summary on the three-step process. Use material from the first three paragraphs of page 174, the first paragraph on page 181, and the first three paragraphs of day 5 on page 186, all in the member's book. As you present this summary, point out the three placards with the three key words.

Group Sharing Time (30 minutes)

1. Remind the group members of their very important exercises concerning identification. The first exercise dealt with identifying feelings. Say: "Feelings often help us know problems exist before we know what the problems are."

Discuss the exercises on page 176 in the member's book. Encourage members to share new insights about feelings from this week's study.

Share the answers recorded in the margin box of the member's book to question 3 on page 179.

2. Say: "In the study from day 2 you worked to identify situations with certain feelings, thoughts, or words; black-and-white thinking and actions characteristic of codependency. Then, in an exercise at the top of page 183 in your book, you used one of these four situations to practice detaching."

Pause for the group members to change their seating so that the wall with "Detach" on it becomes the focal wall. Ask members to turn to page 183 in their books.

Ask group members to find partners. Ask each partner to choose another situation from the exercises recorded on page 180. Then ask partners to take turns asking and answering several of the questions at the top of page 182 and at the top of page 183. These detachment questions help clarify difficult situations. The listening partner should ask clarifying questions and encourage the detaching process but should not interject personal judgments on what the partner is saying.

Call time after 10 minutes. Without sharing specifics of any situation, invite those who are willing to share insights about themselves and about the process of detaching. Allow time for individuals to affirm their partners' work in the exercise.

3. Ask and discuss: "How do you feel about the step of detaching?" To emphasize the importance of the second step read aloud the first paragraph on page 181 in the member's book.

Invite group members to share responses they wrote in the margin box on page 185. As various principles are mentioned, remind group members about key points on detaching found in the day 4 material.

Small-Group Sharing Time (25 minutes)

1. Ask members to rejoin their partners and turn to the wall displaying the "Decide" placard. Ask partners to review the memory verses together and to use them as the basis of a prayer for the work of step three—deciding.

2. Give each group member a copy of Worksheet 10. Instruct partners to discuss two of the situations you identified on page 180 of the member's book and to help each other formulate specific, practical decisions which will help them act in healthy ways in this situation. Allow at least 15 minutes for this activity.

If time allows, ask all the group members to share their decisions. Encourage them to keep this worksheet with them and use it to bolster their commitment to these decisions.

Closure (20 minutes)

1. Distribute Worksheet 11. Allow several minutes for individual work.

Call time. Encourage the group members to share with one another their fears about the three-step process and releasing past dysfunction. Then, ask them to share benefits they identified. At this point encourage any person who made a drawing for the second written exercise on page 188 in the member's book to explain it to the group. Affirm the insights these drawings represent about recovery.

2. Briefly preview unit 11. Caution that some members may feel it is a step backward to study grief during a unit, but emphasize that grief is an essential step to recovery involving a great commitment of honesty and objectivity. Ask group members to think of an object they can bring to next week's session symbolizing any grieving they recently have done or need to do. Encourage them to call you before the group session if they have difficulty with this assignment.

3. Conclude by symbolizing the group's commitment to the three-step process through prayer. Use one of the following options to close the group process through prayer.

Option 1: Join hands and form a circle. Stretch the circle wide until only fingertips are touching. Begin an open-eyed, heads-up prayer. Invite the group members to add sentence prayers when you indicate:

"Lord, we thank You for leading us to this point in our study and for showing us the hope of change, healing, and recovery. We commit ourselves to taking the first step (pause while everyone takes one step toward the center of the circle), and we are willing to *identify* in our lives ... (allow time for group members to add personal sentence prayers). We commit ourselves to taking the second step (pause while everyone takes another step toward the center of the circle), and we are willing to *detach* from these things in our lives ... (allow time for group members to add personal sentence prayers). We commit ourselves to taking the third step (pause while everyone takes one last step toward the center of the circle; members are close enough now to drape arms over shoulders or around waists), and we are willing to *decide* for our lives ... (allow time for group members to add personal sentence prayers). With Jesus' help and for His sake, Amen."

Option 2: Stand and join hands. Lead a time of directed prayer. Begin the prayer with praise and gratitude to God for the group. Next pray, "Father we thank You for the difficult truth You are leading us to *identify* in and about our lives." (Permit a time of silence for group members to identify and express their prayers aloud or silently.) "We thank You for leading us to become willing and able to *detach* from these issues in our lives." (Allow a time of silent or spoken response to God.) "We ask that You give us the courage and wisdom necessary to *decide* on new and Christ-honoring patterns for our lives." (Give members time to pray.) Conclude the time of prayer as you feel appropriate, with your own words, the Lord's prayer, or a song.

After the Session

❏ Read "Before the Session" for Group Session 11 (on the following page) to evaluate the amount of preparation you will need for your next group session. Record at the top of the Group Session 11 material a time when you will do your preparation.
❏ Study carefully unit 11 and do all the exercises in the member's book.
❏ Early in the week call or send reminder cards to group members about the assignment made during closure.

Group Session 11

Learning to Grieve

Session Goals

This session is designed to help members—
  accept the importance of grief in recovery;
  understand the difficulty, but importance, of objectivity about personal issues and experiences;
  identify, describe, and feel the emotions associated with grief experiences;
  support and encourage each other in sharing about grief.

Before the Session

❑ Gather two large sheets of newsprint. Label one "Grief is . . ." and the other "Grief is not . . . ." Attach them to a focal wall inside your room. Tape several markers on the wall beside each one.
❑ Collect a large candle, candle holder, and matches for use during the session.
❑ Take to the session an item which represents a type of grief in your own life. (During the last session you asked your group members to bring their own symbol of grief.)
❑ Gather this week's front-page sections of your local newspaper. Place these sections on a large table in the room.
❑ Use your church media library to gather resources on Christian responses to and understanding of anger. Display these in your group session room.

You may want to check with your church staff or a local Christian counselor for recommendations on resources, classes, workshops, or support groups available for those learning to manage anger. Be prepared to share this information with your group. After the session be available for one-on-one consultation with interested group members.

During the Session

Introductory Activity (20 minutes)

1. As members arrive ask them to go to the "Grief" posters and to fill in their thoughts after they read the statements, "Grief is . . ." and "Grief is not . . . ."

2. Then, ask group members to move to the table with the newspapers on it. Ask members to tear out one article that most captures their attention and interest.

3. Gather in the circle. Ask group members to examine the article they've torn from the newspaper. Ask: "If you had been assigned to cover this story and to write this article, could you be objective about it? Explain your answer."

Listen to a few responses. Emphasize that many times people find difficulty in being objective about newspaper stories such as these when the story's topic offends their morals or involves their feelings, when they are emotionally tied to a person or place the story mentions, or when they in some other way find themselves caught up in the drama of the situation.

Remark that the task of being objective about yourself almost seems to be an impossible one. Refer group members to the diagram on page 192 in their books. Say: "Once you begin to take the courageous step of telling the truth about yourself, others, your feelings, your behaviors, and their consequences, you are practicing **objectivity** However, honesty about deep wounds does not bring immediate relief; more likely, it brings grief. For the first time you may be acknowledging what you've lost while codependency trapped you. Some of you have lost portions of your childhood, your ability to trust others, or your belief in your own worth and lovableness; maybe you've lost key relationships through abandonment, divorce, or death. If you've struggled at all with the issues of codependency, then you have something to grieve."

4. Pause for a time of prayer. Direct a prayer experience while group members pray silently. Group members may want to hold hands. Use the following statements to direct the prayer. Pause between these statements for silent prayer.
  Something of what I've just said may have prompted a powerful emotion inside you. Tell the Lord how you feel at this moment.
  Some of you finally may have acknowledged to yourselves that a tangled relationship has wounded you. Tell the Lord about your wounds.
  Some of you just now are realizing how much you need the Lord's intervention in your life. Confess to Him your need and praise Him for possessing the wisdom to meet your need.
  Some of you are feeling overwhelmed again by how much you need the support of this group, and perhaps

you are a bit panicked because we're so near the end of this study. Thank God for this group, and ask Him to show you where your support will be when these group sessions end.

After a few more moments of silence, close this prayer. After the prayer be sensitive to anyone who is struggling for composure or who obviously is moved. If necessary take time to debrief feelings and insights.

Discovery-Group Sharing Time (25 minutes)

1. Refer group members again to the diagram on page 192 in the member's book. Instruct them to take a pencil or pen and to shade in the door marked "Objectivity" to show how much objectivity they have about themselves and about their recovery needs. Pause a moment. Then remark: "If you shaded the door a little bit, this probably represents the fact that you still are denying your need to recover from the wounds and tangled relationships of codependency. The more you shaded the door, the more objective you may feel about yourself and the more likely you'll be to do the work of grieving and recovering." To discuss what grief is and what it is not, mention statements members wrote on the two sheets of newsprint.

2. Say: "Of all the steps in the grief process, probably the most troublesome is anger. Whether or not it is connected to grief, anger is the emotion that we are leery of and do not trust. If understanding your anger and how to express it is an ongoing issue for you, you've not found all the help you need as you worked in day 3 of this unit. I encourage you to take time to learn about anger and how to manage it in your life." Refer to any resources you may have brought or to any other helps for dealing with anger you've identified. Indicate that you are available to talk about this in a one-on-one manner after the session.

Ask group members to turn to the first written exercise on page 199 in the member's book. Use their responses to discuss anger, its sources in deep wounds, and the role of anger in completing the grief process.

3. Remark that the comfort identified in the unit memory verses may be the comfort group members need as they admit they are angry people. Encourage several members to recite the memory verses.

Ask members to give testimonies about what comfort means to them in these verses. Conclude by asking group members to share responses they recorded to the written exercise in the middle of page 201 in their books.

Closure (45 minutes)

1. Ask group members to come back together. Light the candle and place it in the center of the group. Read John 11:1-6, 17-44. Tell the group this passage is one of the most beautiful stories from Jesus' life.

In it we learn that Jesus grieved with two sisters who lost a brother. Jesus also grieved about His own loss of His friend, Lazarus. We also learn that times of grief can be times when we see the glory of God (v. 40).

Say: "As we close this session, we want to consider the gift of grief. Grief is vital to the healing experience but grief is painful. You brought with you objects that symbolize your recent grief. I invite you to share what you've brought, why you've brought it, and where you are now in your grief experience. Do you see grief as a good gift at this time in your life? Why or why not?"

As much as possible, let group members be their own encouragement to each other. You can participate by sharing just like the other group members do. This is not a teaching moment as much as it is a cathartic, clarifying experience.

The dim, candle-lit room provides some privacy for those who may feel and express deep grief. This setting also prompts group members to listen more carefully to what people say and mean.

2. Ask the Holy Spirit to help you know how to pray to conclude this session.

After the Session

❏ Carefully review the notes you took during this group. Evaluate key topics and needs identified during group sessions. Redesign the lesson plan to include any subjects that, based on your observations of your group, need additional time.

Group Session 12

New Ways of Relating

Session Goals

This session is designed to help members—
share key decisions they have made during the group;
valuate the meaning of the group experience to them;
say goodbye to each other by offering a blessing.

Before the Session

❏ Decide if your room is large enough for the closure activity. If not, reserve a nearby room.
❏ Make copies of the Christian Growth Study Plan form at the end of this leader's guide.
❏ Make two placards. Write one of the following questions on each: "Why have I been here?" and "What personal goal have I accomplished by being here?"
❏ Use the final worksheet master to make Bible markers for group members. Copy these onto heavier paper. If you have time, you may want to add ribbon or yarn, or you may want to write a personal message on the back.

During the Session

OPTIONAL NOTE: As you plan for Group Session 12, you may want to leave this final session basically unstructured. You might ask a few discussion questions or use the Unit Review on page 223 in the member's book to prompt discussion. You know your comfort level as leader, and you know the personality of your group. If the final session is best conducted in an unstructured way for you and your group, be bold enough to choose this approach!

Introductory Activity (30 minutes)

1. As group members enter, ask them to fill out the Christian Growth Study Plan forms for this course. Briefly explain the Christian Growth Study Plan system for those who are unfamiliar with the system.

2. Ask everyone to join the circle. Remind members that you began the group 12 weeks ago by asking two questions: "Why am I here?" and "What personal goal can I accomplish by being here?" Say: "Tonight we need to revise those questions and to ask them again." Display the two placards. Invite persons who are willing to share their answers to one or both questions. This sharing should be a time for celebration, affirmation, and encouragement. Allow the group to perform these functions for its members.

3. Refer group members to the unit review on page 223 in their books. Provide time for anyone to share what he or she has written.

4. Raise the issue of whether the group members want to continue meeting on a regular, informal basis as a support for one another. Do not, however, pressure any group member to continue meeting. Members might choose to meet once a month after church or for a potluck supper. If they choose to set a date for the first follow-up meeting, tell the group the only structured item for that meeting will be to negotiate a new contract. In the contract members would agree on details such as how often to conduct these informal gatherings, where to meet, and how long to meet.

Closure (1 hour)

1. Push back against the walls all furniture in your room. Inform the group that you are setting up a trust experience to prompt them to share with each other final thoughts about the discovery-group experience.

Tell the group members that they will repeat the experience several times so that they will play the different parts involved: two ships lost at sea; two lighthouses, rocks and obstacles, the wind, and the waves.

Enlist two volunteers and blindfold them; they are to be the ships lost at sea. Enlist two others to be lighthouses. Move the lighthouses to remote parts of the room apart from each other. Allow each lighthouse to speak to its ship so the ship can identify the sound of its lighthouse. Ask two additional volunteers to be the wind and the waves. The remaining group members scatter out between the lost ships and the lighthouses. Rocks may crouch on the ground. Several may choose to chain with each other to form a difficult obstacle. Once the rocks and obstacles assume a position, they may not move.

At the beginning of the exercise and at various impromptu times during it, instruct the wind and the waves to turn or gently spin the ships to disorient them. Ask the lighthouses to offer instructions to the ships to avoid the obstacles and to reach the safety of the lighthouse.

This is not a race between the two ships. When each ship reaches the lighthouse, the exercise begins again with group members changing roles.

2. After several repeats of the exercise, call group members back to the circle. Say: "Imagine that you've been acting out the journey of discovery you've been on for these past weeks in our *Untangling Relationships* group."

Ask and prompt discussion of the following debriefing questions:
   Which part that you played is most like the role you've had in this group?
   Or, which part that you played is most like the discovery journey you've been on these past 11 or 12 weeks?
   Think carefully: Before this course began, which experience did you prefer—that of the storm or the lighthouse's safety? Now that the course is concluding, which do you prefer—the storm or safety?

(NOTE: These are not trick questions! Some members genuinely may prefer the storm; they gain a lot of personal power and pity from others for their distress, and they never have to confront the difficult obstacles. Before they began the course some may have preferred safety. Their safety was that of not admitting to deep wounds and tangled relationships. They lived life as if all is well. The storm for this person represents telling the truth and bearing the consequences of objectivity.)

   Imagine that the lighthouse is the Lord. How close are you to Him today? What will happen when you actually rest in the safety He offers you?
   Recite the memory verse together. Ask: "How do you feel about the promise that God will complete his work in you-that He will get you safely to shore?"

3. Say: "The most important things any group will do is say hello and say goodbye. If we lived in Old England, goodbye would have been said, 'God be with you.' As we prepare to leave, let's say goodbye to each other in a way that offers the hope of God's blessing to each other. I'll call each of your names and pause. If you have a word of blessing or goodbye for that person, speak it then. Try to be succinct and to the point so everyone who wants to share gets the chance."

Facilitate this final experience of blessing and farewell. Be sure to call your name and the apprentice's name, too.

4. Join hands and pray or sing together to dismiss. Plan to do this in a way that will be most meaningful to your group. Distribute the Bible markers.

After the Session

❑ Plan to send each group member a personal letter within a week of this session. Affirm decisions they made and contributions they made to the group. Remind them of the follow-up group meeting if your group decided to do this.
❑ Make a copy of Leader Worksheet, "Evaluating Each Session." Use this to assess the final session. If you have an apprentice, complete and discuss this worksheet with him or her. Use this final evaluation session to debrief the entire group experience. Make notes that would be helpful to someone who leads a subsequent group. Give these to the person who enlisted you as group leader.

Notes

[1] This activity adapted from "Trust," in Sharon Baack, Hal Hill, and Joe Palmer, *Adventure Recreation: An Adventure in Group Building* (Nashville: Convention Press, 1989), 69.

Made in United States
Troutdale, OR
05/15/2024

19894747R00018